COSTA RICA

A TRUE BOOK®
by
Kathleen W. Deady

Children's Press®
A Division of Scholastic Inc.

New York Toronto London Auckland Sydney
Mexico City New Delhi Hong Kong
Danbury, Connecticut

The lush landscape of
Tabacon Hot Springs

Reading Consultant
Sonja I. Smith
Reading Specialist

Content Consultant
Dr. Amy J. Johnson, Ph.D.
Berry College

Library of Congress Cataloging-in-Publication Data

Deady, Kathleen W.
   Costa Rica / Kathleen W. Deady.
        p. cm. — (A true book)
Includes bibliographical references and index.
Contents: Land—An endangered environment—Settlement to
independence—Developing democracy—Everyday life—Celebrations
and recreation.
   ISBN 0-516-22810-2 (lib. bdg.)   0-516-25831-1 (pbk.)
1. Costa Rica—Juvenile literature. [1. Costa Rica.] I. Title. II. Series.
F1543.2.D43 2004
972.86—dc22

                                              2003018661

CHILDREN'S PRESS, and A TRUE BOOK™, and associated logos are
trademarks and or registered trademarks of Scholastic Library Publishing.
SCHOLASTIC and associated logos are trademarks and or registered
trademarks of Scholastic Inc.
   2 3 4 5 6 7 8 9 10 R 13 12 11 10 09 08 07 06

Contents

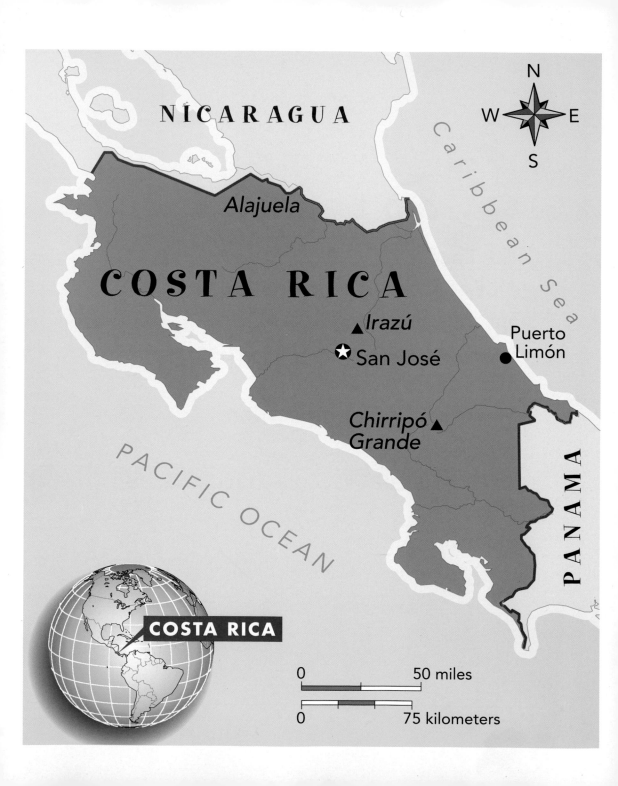

The Land

Costa Rica is a small country in Central America. Central America also includes Guatemala, Belize, Honduras, El Salvador, Nicaragua, and Panama. These seven countries form a bridge of land called an **isthmus**. They connect North and South America. The vast

Pacific Ocean lies southwest of Costa Rica. Costa Rica's northeast coast borders the Caribbean Sea. Panama is southeast and Nicaragua is to the north.

Mountains cover much of Costa Rica's interior. Several mountain ranges together form a chain of mountains called the Cordilleras in Spanish, which is the official language of Costa Rica. The Cordilleras cut from southeast to northwest through central

Mountains cover much of Costa Rica.

Costa Rica. Chirripó Grande, at 12,530 feet (3,819 meters), is the tallest peak.

Costa Rica's mountains are part of the Ring of Fire. This line of volcanoes circles much

Irazú volcano

of the Pacific Ocean. Irazú is the highest of Costa Rica's several active volcanoes.

In the middle of these mountains is a highland **plateau** called Meseta Central, Spanish for "central plateau." About three-quarters of the nearly four million Costa Ricans live in this area. Nestled there, only a short distance from Irazú, is San José. It is the capital and largest city.

The mountains and Meseta Central separate two lowland

The city of San José is surrounded by mountains.

Visitors enjoy beautiful beaches at Corcovado National Park.

areas. The Caribbean lowlands spread to the east coast along the Caribbean Sea. The Pacific coastal strip reaches the Pacific Ocean on the west coast. Tropical rain forests cover parts of these coastal plains. Miles of sandy beaches line both shores.

An Endangered Environment

Costa Rica's environment is rich in plant and animal life. Its large, unique animal population is partly due to its location. Many animals from North and South America live side by side in Costa Rica. As a result, its forests support about six in every one hundred of the world's animals.

A tropical rain forest
near Puerto Viejo

Costa Rica has several types
of forests. Steamy rain forests
are found along the Caribbean

lowlands and in the southwest. These areas get anywhere from 160 to 350 inches (406 to 889 centimeters) of rain yearly. Their closeness to the equator keeps them about 75 degrees Fahrenheit (24 degrees Celsius) all year round.

The northwest has tropical dry forests that have much longer dry periods. Cloud forests are at higher elevations where warm, humid air meets cooler mountain air.

Tiny squirrel monkeys (left) are the rarest and most endangered of Costa Rica's monkeys. The keel-billed toucan (right) sports a rainbow-colored bill.

Tapirs, monkeys, sloths, and anteaters all live in Costa Rica's forests. Large cats include jaguars, margays, and pumas. Toucans, parrots, and the rare quetzal fly overhead.

Poison arrow frogs, iguanas, crocodiles, insects, and butter-flies are everywhere.

Thousands of kinds of plants thrive in Costa Rica's climate. Dazzling orchids, the national flower, fill the rain forests.

A black orchid

Palm trees and mangroves grow in coastal areas. Leafy trees, including purple jacaranda and meadow oaks, color the drier forests.

Today, these forests are in danger of being destroyed. For years, farmers have cleared land to grow crops. Ranchers have cut trees to provide grazing land for their cattle. As forests are destroyed, so are animal homes. The destruction of animal habitats means that many animals are in danger of dying out.

In the past, many of Costa Rica's forests were cleared to make room for farms or ranchland.

Costa Ricans are working to save their environment. Many parts of Costa Rica have been declared national forests. This means that people are not allowed to destroy the forests.

A group of students takes an ecotour of the Tortuguero canal system.

Ecotourism is a growing industry in Costa Rica. Tourists, or visitors, are encouraged to explore the environment without harming it. They also learn ways to help save the environment, such as not feeding animals in the wild.

Settlement to Independence

Scientists believe the first people lived in Costa Rica around ten thousand years ago. These early people hunted and fished. They ate fruits and berries and learned to farm.

Europeans began exploring the Americas in the late 1400s. In 1502, Christopher Columbus,

representing Spain, reached the
coast of Costa Rica. The American
Indians who greeted Columbus
wore jewelry. They gave him gifts
of gold. Columbus believed the
area had great wealth. It was later

named Costa Rica, which means "rich coast" in Spanish.

Rumors of great wealth brought other Spanish explorers. They soon discovered there was little gold or other minerals, and many explorers left. Those who stayed tried to make the Indians

After the arrival of the Spanish, many Native Americans fled into the forests.

their slaves and force them to work. Some Indians fled to the mountains or died fighting. Many Indians also died of diseases that were unknowingly brought to the area by the Spanish.

In 1562, Juan Vásquez de Coronado started the first permanent Spanish settlement at Cartago. The settlers farmed their own land. Because Costa Rica was poor, Spain paid it little attention. During this time, Costa Rica grew slowly as a peaceful colony. By the 1700s,

Costa Rica grew slowly and peacefully, with small ranches and farms.

new settlements spread westward into the central plateau.

In 1821, the colonies in Central America began breaking away from Spanish rule. Costa Rica became independent from Spain on September 15, 1821.

The Road to Democracy

In the 1800s, leaders made changes that helped Costa Rica's **economy** grow. President Juan Mora Fernandez built homes and schools. He also gave people land in the central plateau. The climate and soil there were rich with volcanic ash. These conditions were perfect for growing

Coffee plantation owners hired large numbers of people to work the land.

coffee. Coffee became a major crop for export, or sale to other countries. It was a huge boost to the economy.

Juan Rafael Mora Porras was president from 1849 to 1859. Porras started Costa Rica's first national bank and many public schools. He also established the first system of streetlights.

From 1870 to 1882, General Tomas Guardia seized control. Guardia was a military **dictator**. He ruled harshly and restricted freedoms. However, he also had ideas that helped Costa Rica. Guardia improved

San José in 1859

schools and public health and cleanliness. He also built the first railroad in Central America, the Atlantic Railroad.

Jungle Train

The railroad made it easier to carry huge numbers of bananas out of the forests and sell them to faraway markets.

Between 1871 and 1890, thousands of people came from Great Britain, Italy, China, and Jamaica to build the Atlantic Railroad. It was nicknamed the Jungle Train. The train ran from Meseta Central through the dense rain forests to the Caribbean coast. It greatly improved travel, the transport of goods such as bananas and coffee, and economic development.

Rafael Angel Calderón Guardia and his wife on a trip to the United States in 1940

The 1900s brought mostly improvements and progress toward **democracy**. In the 1940s, President Rafael Angel Calderón Guardia had ideas for many changes. He worked to expand health care and started

Costa Ricans prepare for civil war. Although the war only lasted a few weeks, more than 2,000 people were killed.

reforms for workers, such as better wages. But there were some problems. In 1948, strong disagreement with his ideas led to the worst civil war in Costa Rica's history. Also, from 1963 to

1965, eruptions of Irazú caused damage to crops and economic problems for the people.

Popular President José "Don Pepe" Figueres Ferrer led from 1953 to 1958 and again from

"Don Pepe" Figueres

1970 to 1974. He worked for civil rights, such as women's right to vote. He set limits on terms for presidents and worked hard to build democracy in Costa Rica.

In recent years, Costa Ricans have been working hard to rebuild a weak economy. They have made much progress in creating a democracy. Today, Costa Rica is a success story in Central America.

Everyday Life

Costa Ricans call themselves Ticos. About ninety-five in every one hundred people are white or mestizo. Whites **descend** from European **ancestors**, mostly from Spain. Mestizos are of mixed Spanish and Indian descent. Costa Rica has a small number of Asians, Indians, and blacks of

Jamaican descent. Spanish is the official language, although many people speak some English.

Education has always been important. About ninety-six in every one hundred people can read. Schools are free, and children are required to attend school until ninth grade.

A classroom in Costa Rica

San José is filled with food, crafts, and other goods for sale.

Cities are fast-paced and crowded with cars and street vendors selling goods. Many people live in wooden houses or concrete or brick apartment buildings. Poorer people live in crowded apartments at the edges of the cities. Wealthy people have large ranch or Spanish-style homes.

In rural areas, country homes are made of wood and painted bright colors. Others are small cottages made of sun-dried clay bricks called adobe. Rural areas have fewer paved roads and sidewalks than the cities. Some have less running water and electricity.

Costa Rica's economy is still based largely on farming. Many people work in the coffee industry. Farmers grow bananas on plantations in the tropical lowlands.

Factories make processed foods, tobacco products, and

More than half of all Costa Ricans live in rural areas (above). A worker rakes coffee beans to ensure that they dry evenly (right).

clothing. Technology and tourism have also been growing in recent years. Technology produces goods such as electronics and medical equipment.

Celebrations and Recreation

Ticos enjoy celebrations and festivals, or fiestas, throughout the year. Music and dance are important parts of most festivals. Musicians play guitars and large instruments called marimbas. People wear colorful costumes and dance in the streets.

A traditional marimba band

Bullfights, rodeos, and food are popular at local fairs and fiestas.

Ticos celebrate several religious holidays. Most Costa Ricans are Roman Catholic. Easter celebrations include fireworks and dancing. Street processions act out religious

events. Many towns have colorful festivals honoring a **patron saint**. On August 2, Our Lady of the Angels honors La Negrita, the patron saint of Costa Rica.

Some celebrations are for national holidays. October 12 is

Columbus Day, called El Día de la Raza, which means "the day of the race." In a weeklong carnival, Costa Ricans celebrate the different races of people that make up Central America. On September 15, Ticos celebrate Independence Day with parades, parties, and flag waving.

Costa Ricans enjoy parades, music, and dancing.

Costa Ricans are passionate about soccer.

Costa Ricans enjoy many sports. Children play soccer, the national sport, anywhere and at any time. Bicycling and boxing, as well as basketball, tennis, baseball, and golf, are popular. Ticos also enjoy water sports. The Pacific coast is especially good for surfing.

Oxcart Folk Art

An artisan paints colorful designs on an oxcart.

Before the Jungle Train, people used oxcarts to carry coffee beans through the mountains to the coast for export. The sturdy oxcart, or carreta, had solid wheels with no spokes. People started painting brightly colored designs on the wheels, and over time, oxcart painting became very popular. Today, the oxcart is a national symbol. The second Sunday in March is Dia del Boyero (Oxcart Driver's Day). Oxcart drivers from around the country come to San Antonio de Escazu to take part in colorful oxcart parades through town.

To Find Out More

Here are some additional resources to help you learn more about Costa Rica.

 **Books**

Fisher, Frederick. **Festivals of the World: Costa Rica.** Gareth Stevens Publishing, 1999.

Moritz, Patricia M. **Costa Rica.** The Rourke Book Company, 2002.

Shields, Charles. **Costa Rica.** Mason Crest Publishers, 2002.

Sneed, Collard, III. **The Forest in the Clouds.** Charlesbridge Publishing, 2000.

West, Tracy. **Costa Rica.** Carolrhoda Books, Inc. 1999.

Organizations and Online Sites

Costa Rica: No Artificial Ingredients
http://www.tourism-costarica.com

This official site of the Costa Rica Tourist Board has a broad range of information and pictures, especially on nature and wildlife.

General Information about Costa Rica
http://www.horizontes.com/general_info/

Learn about Costa Rican holidays, food, national parks, wildlife and more.

InfoCostaRica.com
http://www.infocostarica.com/general/

Find lots of general information, see pictures of wildlife, and even learn some Spanish.

Science in the Rain Forest
http://www.pbs.org/tal/costa_rica/index.html

Take a walk in the rain forest and learn lots of interesting facts.

Important Words

ancestors relatives who lived a long time ago

democracy a form of government in which the people choose their leaders in elections

descend originate from

dictator a ruler with absolute authority to control and govern a country

economy a country's wealth, based on the products and services it provides

isthmus a narrow area of land that connects two larger landmasses

patron saint a saint who is thought to protect a nation or group

plateau a raised area of land

Index

Meet the Author

Kathleen W. Deady has written more than thirty books for children. They include picture books and non-fiction on a variety of topics. Her work has also appeared in several children's magazines. She has worked as a preschool teacher and director, as well as a special education tutor in elementary schools.

Kathleen lives in Manchester, New Hampshire, with her husband Bill, daughter Erin, and son Matthew. When she isn't writing, she enjoys singing in a local women's singing group, as well as gardening, camping, biking, and feeding birds.

Photographs © 2004: AP/Wide World Photos: 40 (Kent Gilbert), 28, 31; Archive Photos/Getty Images: 28; Bridgeman Art Library International Ltd., London/New York/Metropolitan Museum of Art, New York, USA: 20; Buddy Mays/Travel Stock: 17, 43; Corbis Images: 25, 30 (Bettmann), 7 (Gary Braasch), 23; D. Donne Bryant Stock Photography: 42; Dave G. Houser/HouserStock, Inc.: 2 (Ellen Barone), 10, 35, 39; Herb Swanson: 34; Kevin Schafer: 8, 9, 14 right, 15; Larry Ulrich Stock Photography Inc.: 14 left (Tom Blagden), 12; North Wind Picture Archives: 21; Robert Fried Photography: cover, 37 left; South American Pictures: 37 right (Robert Francis), 18 (Rebecca Whitfield); Stock Montage, Inc.: 26; The Image Works: 1 (Sonda Dawes); Woodfin Camp & Associates: 41
Map by Bob Italiano.